PRAYING
FOR YOUR
WIFE

DEVOTIONAL & PRAYER JOURNAL

KINGSLEY OKONKWO

PRAYING FOR YOUR WIFE
(DEVOTIONAL AND PRAYER JOURNAL)
Copyright © 2022 Kingsley Okonkwo
ISBN 9798364256041

All rights reserved. No portion of this publication may be reproduced or stored in retrieval system or transmitted in any form or by any means- electronic, mechanical, photocopy or any other without the permission of the author.

Published & Printed By:
MillionValues Concepts
105, Igi-Olugbin, Pedro,
Lagos
Tel: 08185710897
Email: millionvalues@gmail.com

Cover Design by
Designs by Femmy

CONTENTS

Dedication 5
Note To Reader 7
Day 1: What Do You Call Her? 11
Day 2: Her Everyday Affairs Prosper 17
Day 3: Above All – Be In Health 23
Day 4: Above All – Soul Prosperity 29
Day 5: Unlocking Favour 35
Day 6: A Wise Woman 41
Day 7: A Sound Mind 47
Day 8: No Fear 53
Day 9: Eyes That See 59
Day 10: Seasoned Speech 65
Day 11: Restored Soul – After All The
    Stress Of The Day 71
Day 12: No Sorrow 77
Day 13: Grace To Build 83
Day 14: Fruitful Vine 89
Day 15: Inner Strength 95
Day 16: Finances 101
Day 17: Multitask Efficiently 107

Day 18: She Will Prophesy 113

Day 19: Her Understanding Enlightened **119**
Day 20: Unholy Alliances **125**
Day 21: Her Conversations **131**
Day 22: Pillar Not A Caterpillar **137**
Day 23: Help **143**
Day 24: Peace And No Worry **149**
Day 25: None Of These Diseases **155**
Day 26: Call Her Blessed **161**
Day 27: Exempt From Hustle **167**
Day 28: Health And Healing **173**
Day 29: Every Need Supplied **179**
Day 30: Even When She Sleeps **185**
Day 31: A Guarded Heart **191**
Bonus: A Faithful Wife **197**
Author's Profile **202**

DEDICATION

To Mildred,
My ever-praying personal prophetess and prayer warrior, you make prayer real and enjoyable and you have taught many all over the world to do the same.
I'm so proud of you and I will forever pray for you.
Continue to colour this world with your God flavour.

NOTE TO READER

"MEN ought always to pray and not get tired"

The world, the church and the homes are in dire need of men who pray. There are so many reasons why, for instance in a home God has appointed the man as the Head, meaning in terms of jurisdiction his prayer has a very powerful effect over his wife and kids; in fact you will see in Acts 18, Cornelius spoke for him and his house without asking them; he had the spiritual jurisdiction to do so.

Then he led Paul and Silas outside and asked, "What must I do to be saved?" They answered, "Believe in the Lord Jesus and you will be saved—you and all your family." Then they prophesied the word of the Lord over him and all his family. Even though the hour was late, he washed their wounds. Then he and all his family were baptized. He took Paul and Silas into his home and set them at his table and fed them. The jailer and all his family were filled with joy in their new found faith in God.
—**Acts 16: 30-34 TPT**

To My Dear Reader

I believe God that this book will stir married men everywhere to take their place spiritually in their homes, and pray for their wives. I know most men want a praying wife, but ALL wives NEED a praying husband.

Let's pray.

–Kingsley Okonkwo.

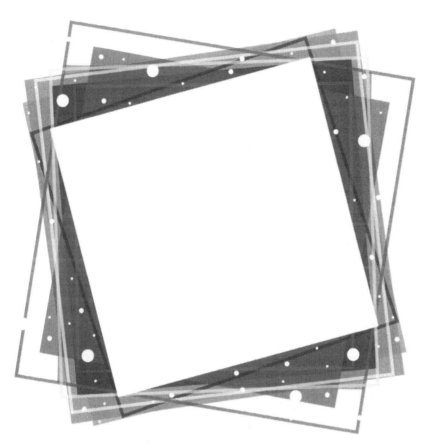

Action: print and paste a picture of your wife.

This is _____ the Love of my life, the queen of my heart, the gift of God to me. I make a commitment to pray for her every day till she becomes all that God has destined for her to be.

—01— WHAT DO YOU CALL HER?

> *Then the Lord God said, "It is not good for the man to be alone. I will make a helper who is right for him."*
> *The Lord God had formed all the wild animals and all the birds out of the ground. Then he brought them to the man to see what he would call them. Whatever the man called each creature became its name.*
>
> *—Genesis 2:18-19 GWT*

After God made man, He determined that it was not good for the man to be alone.

He needed a helper that was perfect for him; one that would be comparable to him but also suitable for and adaptable to him. So God made different animals and brought them to the man and the Bible is very clear on the fact that what the man called them is what they became.

This scripture is a foundation for how marriage began and it can also work as a blueprint for how marriage should be. This tells me that the words you speak over your wife are very crucial. The words you speak to her personally and the words you speak over her in the place of prayer. What names are you calling her in prayer? What names are you declaring over her?

Remember life and death are in the power of the tongue, meaning the tongue can speak words that bring life or cause death. Instead of complaining about your wife or saying negative things about her, speak life over her and she will live.

WORKSHEET

Write out as many qualities as you want to see in your wife.

These are the qualities you will call your wife in prayer daily and I guarantee you that in accordance with scripture this is what she will become.

PRAYER POINTS

- **Pray that your words will mould your wife into the woman that God created her to be.**
- **Pray that whatever name you call her according to the word of God is what will find full expression in her life.**

DECLARATION

I declare that *(insert your wife's name)* is blessed. She is a virtuous woman and an excellent reference for younger women/wives. She is indeed my crown. She walks in divine health and is blessed with a sound mind and judgement. She flourishes financially. She walks in the fullness of her calling with no holds barred. She fulfils destiny and ultimately makes You proud, in Jesus name.

FURTHER STUDY:
Genesis 17:15 (GW), Genesis 2:23 (MSG)

—02—
HER EVERYDAY AFFAIRS PROSPER

How truly I love you! We're the best of friends, and I pray for good fortune in everything you do, and for your good health—that your everyday affairs prosper.

—3 John 1:2 MSG

*E*veryone wants to prosper. Not only in the big things but also in the everyday little things. The truth is your wife's life is not only made up of big and important things but the simple and even often mundane things. You will be amazed at how stressful her life can become if she does not effectively manage her everyday affairs like caring for the home, the children, herself and even you.

Take the time to pray for every area of her life because it is the little things not handled that now become large things that stress her. Pray for her to have daily victories in every area of her life. Pray for her that she prospers in everything she does.

Praying for her is a sign that you truly love her and knowing what to pray means you are paying attention to her daily needs and desires, which will improve your relationship greatly.

WORKSHEET

Write down the day-to-day activities that stress your wife out when left unattended or that you see her struggling to achieve.

Find out ways you can help her in these areas, and where you can't, pray for her that she is strengthened to achieve them.

PRAYER POINTS

- Pray that God will bless the work of your wife's hands, make her prosperous and give her good fortune in everything she does.
- Pray for God's strength within and upon her to carry out her activities daily.

- Pray that she will not be weighed down by the different seasons of life.

DECLARATION

I declare over my wife *(insert your wife's name)*, that everything in her life goes well: her relationships blossom, her ministry is fruitful, her businesses thrive, in her career she excels, she experiences abundance in her finances, and depth in her spiritual life. She will prosper in everything she does because Your Spirit is at work in her life.

FURTHER STUDY
Psalm 132:15 (BSB), Deuteronomy 28:11-12 (NLT)

—03—
ABOVE ALL – BE IN HEALTH

Beloved friend, I pray that you are prospering in every way and that you continually enjoy good health, just as your soul is prospering.

—3 John 1:2 TPT

The family unit is always under attack by satan. He doesn't just attack the institution of marriage, he attacks the individuals in a marriage; he attacks the men in their finances while women experience the attack mostly in the area of their health. Trust me, you don't want your wife to battle with her health. It will affect her, you, the children, family finances and the general well-being of the family. So what do you do? You take charge in the place of prayer and declare what you want to see happen in her health.

Just like God's word says, it is important that she enjoys health in every way –from the crown of her head to the sole of her feet. Pray for every organ and system in her body that they operate at optimal levels. Every cell, every muscle, every bone, every nerve, her body, her mind, every part of her will be in good health.

You need her to be in good health because a sick wife can be draining; both financially and emotionally.

WORKSHEET

Write down positive confessions you can find in the Word concerning your wife's health.

Declare these confessions over her daily. Remember the Bible says you will have what you say.

PRAYER POINTS

- Pray that your wife will continually enjoy good health and that every organ or system in her body will operate at optimal levels.
- Pray that in accordance with the word of God, your wife is satisfied with long life; she will not die young or before her time.
- Pray that your wife enjoys her long life. Her

household including everyone and everything connected to her enjoys good health.
- Pray that as she receives wealth from God through her works, she will have good health to enjoy it.
- Pray that God will equip her with spiritual, mental and physical strength for her God-given task and He will make her arms strong. That she will always be physically fit.

DECLARATION

Heavenly Father, I thank You for Your finished work on the cross. You took *(insert wife's name)* infirmities and bore her sicknesses, therefore she walks in divine health. Sickness and disease cannot find expression in her body because you took her sickness so she cannot have them any longer. Symptoms don't matter; she is healed. From the crown of her head to the soles of her feet, she is made whole. Every organ and system in her body operates at optimal levels. She enjoys great health, energy and vitality all the days of her long life.

FURTHER STUDY
1 Samuel 25:6 (NIV), Ecclesiastes 5:19 (NLT), Proverbs 31:17 (NIV)

—04—
ABOVE ALL — SOUL PROSPERITY

Beloved, I pray that you may prosper in all things and be in health, just as your soul prospers.

—3 John 1:2 NKJV

*E*very human being is made up of three parts – body, soul and spirit. The body is what we use to stay in touch with the physical realm while the spirit is what connects us to the spirit realm and to God when we become born again. The third part of the human being, which is the soul, is a very vital part that houses our intellect, will and emotions.

3 John 1:2 is so vital when praying for your wife because the woman is such an emotional creature. If her soul prospers it means that she will make sound decisions, she will be able to manage her emotions and she will exhibit self-control. Her soul prospering also determines how her health and other areas fare because with a woman a lot is controlled by her emotions. If she is not doing well emotionally haven't you noticed how it affects her job, her health and her decision-making? So pray for her soul to prosper alongside other areas of her life. Your wife needs soul prosperity and trust me you need it for her too.

WORKSHEET

Write out areas where your wife struggles the most with managing her emotions. Commit these areas to God, call them by name and counter them with God's Word.

PRAYER POINTS

- Pray that your wife prospers in her soul - her emotions, her thoughts and her will and this, in turn, causes her to attract positive things to her life.
- Pray that she has the ability to control her emotions in every circumstance. She will be quick to listen, slow to speak and slow to become angry.
- Pray that depression, anger, unforgiveness and

negative attitudes that damage the soul will not find expression in her.
- Pray that her self-esteem will be healthy and she will have a very healthy self-image.
- Pray that the Holy Spirit works God's word so deep within her soul that whenever she faces challenges it is the word of God that will flow out of her first.
- Pray that she will constantly be a blessing to all that come in contact with her and in return, she will be refreshed herself as she refreshes others.

DECLARATION

I declare that *(insert your wife's name)* has the power to be disciplined in all things. I declare that she is able to manage and control her emotions. She exhibits self-control in every area. Her decisions are always guided by Your word and not by her emotions. She is able to identify the things that are harmful to her and stay away from them. Her words, thoughts and actions are subject to Your Spirit and are acceptable unto you in Jesus name.

FURTHER STUDY
Proverbs 11:25 (BSB)

—05—
UNLOCKING FAVOUR

He who finds a wife finds a good thing and obtains favour from the Lord.

—Proverbs 18:22 NKJV

avour is a very important commodity in life. The things that you get by labour are never comparable to the things you get by favour. Now imagine someone telling you that you can have something in your life that activates that favour continuously. Well, you already do. Your wife is what I like to call your favour pipe. Having her in your life draws favour from God into it.

Your job, now that you have found her, is to recognize her as the good thing that she is; she is blessed and highly favoured by God and your responsibility is to keep that favour activated in the place of prayer. The good part is that as you cultivate that favour the bible says that you will be the first partaker of that fruit of favour in her life. Take it from someone that knows; after I got married everything I was doing simply exploded. This will become your normal – You will find that you will begin to experience acts of kindness around you that are beyond what is due or usual and with little effort, you will find an exponential increase in your life. Now isn't that something worth cultivating?

WORKSHEET

Think about where you were when you got married and how far you've come today. Write out some of the things you have achieved together as a couple.

Now thank God for all these blessings; they will also inspire you to believe for more things together.

PRAYER POINTS

- Pray that your wife will be the first partaker of the favour that she carries and this favour will affect every area of her life.
- Pray that because she is a virtuous woman and a crown to you as her husband that the favour she carries will cause you to reign as king in your field of endeavour.

- Pray that she will constantly bring good and not harm to you and all that is yours, all the days of her life. That she is a favour magnet attracting only good things.
- Pray that among her equals she will always stand out. The Lord surrounds her with favour as a shield and because of this she enjoys preferential treatment always.

DECLARATION

I declare that *(insert your wife's name)* is indeed a good thing and a blessing from the Lord. She complements me and meets me in the areas I need help. I declare that our relationship is strengthened and together, we find Your favour. This union is joined by you Lord, therefore You rule in our affairs. I declare that as she brings favour into my life, she also, enjoys favour all the days of her life In Jesus name.

FURTHER STUDY
2 Timothy 2:6 (HCSB), Proverbs 19:14 (AMP), Luke 1:28 (KJVV), Psalm 5:12 (BSB)

—06—
A WISE WOMAN

If any of you lacks wisdom [to guide him through a decision or circumstance], he is to ask of [our benevolent] God, who gives to everyone generously and without rebuke or blame, and it will be given to him
—James 1:5 AMP

One of the most quoted scriptures when it comes to women is proverbs 14:1 which tells us that *a wise woman builds her home but with her hands the foolish one tears it down.* So much is expected of our wives and the truth is they will need wisdom in large doses if they are to accomplish it all.

Sometimes your wife will need to make decisions or find herself in circumstances that affect the family and she may not have you around at that time to discuss with so pray that she will always access God's wisdom to guide her through. That she will always exhibit her reverence and honour of the Lord by seeking Him first; not friends or people that may give negative counsel. You need to pray that she will be open to receive the wisdom, instruction, and insight that God provides. The wisdom God gives your wife is your safety net because your wife will often give you counsel and knowing her wisdom is from God is the only assurance that she will build your house and not destroy it.

WORKSHEET

Think about a situation where your wife has given you advice that averted trouble or resulted in a better outcome

----

PRAYER POINTS

- Pray that whenever she opens her mouth to speak it will always be the right words; words that bring healing and soothe you and all that hear her.
- Pray that she will always give you godly counsel and this will cause you to soar in life.
- Pray that she will be sensitive to the voice of the Holy Spirit at all times as He teaches her what to do and say and she will not need to take advice from different people.

- God will give her a mouth and wisdom that people will not be able to gainsay.

DECLARATION

I declare that *(insert your wife's name)* is a wise woman and that she exhibits godly wisdom always. She treats people with the love and kindness that You extend to her. She will always live in the consciousness of the fact that she has the Spirit of Truth with her always, and He is able to teach her all things. Her heart will always be receptive to receiving instructions from You in Jesus name.

FURTHER STUDY
Proverbs 31:26 (AMP), 1 John 2:21 (GN)

—07—
A SOUND MIND

For God did not give us a spirit of timidity or cowardice or fear, but [He has given us a spirit] of power and of love and of sound judgement and personal discipline [abilities that result in a calm, well-balanced mind and self-control].

—*2 Tim 1:7 AMP*

I'm sure by now you have discovered how important a woman's mind is to her vital existence. A woman has a mind that is so different from a man's own and her thoughts and emotions usually affect her more than a man can ever understand. One of the best things you can do for her as her husband is to hand her over to the one who understands her since He made her.

Your wife will have great dreams and goals but one of the things she will battle with will be her mind. You need to pray that she only accepts what God is giving her and fear is definitely not one of them. She will need to accept how powerful she is and love herself even when she questions her worth sometimes. Your prayer for her should be that in such times that she will tap into her innate abilities of sound judgement and personal discipline and this will eradicate anxiety so that she will always have a balanced mind and exhibit self control.

The end result would be a life of peace which I'm sure both of you desire.

WORKSHEET

Are there areas of your wife's life where she feels inadequate and has communicated that to you? List them out and take them up in prayer one after the other.

Now go back to the list above and use it to boost her self confidence.

PRAYER POINTS

- Pray that your wife possesses the spirit of power and of love and of sound judgement *and* personal discipline.
- Pray that her love may abound more and more displaying itself in greater depth in real knowledge

and in practical insight, so that she will learn to recognize and treasure what is excellent, identifying the best, and distinguishing moral differences.
- Pray that God will make her of quick understanding in the fear of the LORD and she will not judge after the sight of his eyes, neither reprove after the hearing of her ears.
- Pray that she has the mind of Christ and she understands all things.

DECLARATION

I declare that *(insert your wife's name)* has a sound mind. I break every stronghold and limitation off of her mind. She begins to see as You see, think as You think and speak as You speak. Her mind is renewed. I declare that her mind is stable. I remove every negative thinking pattern. In the moments where her thoughts feel like they are out of control, You would take control and remind her that you have given her a sound mind, in Jesus name.

FURTHER STUDY
Philippians 1:9-10 (AMP), Isaiah 11:3 (KJV), 1 Corinthians 2:16 (NLT)

—08—
NO FEAR

For God did not give us a spirit of timidity (of cowardice, of craven and cringing and fawning fear), but [He has given us a spirit] of power and of love and of calm and well-balanced mind and discipline and self-control.

—2 Tim 1:7 AMPC

Life requires boldness. Even if you read through the bible you will find God's response to fear is always to dispel it. God is anti-fear and we should be too.

As her husband, you stand as a priest over her so if at any point you notice that the spirit of fear wants to interfere with the great things you know your wife is called to do then you need to step in and cast out that spirit of fear. If you notice any form of timidity or cowardice then you need to address it in the place of prayer as well. And even when she's faced with situations that should naturally elicit fear she will not give in to it.

At this point, I must be fair and mention that there are usually a lot of situations that may try to steal her peace and cause her anxiety, and she may even try to justify it. Be like Jesus in her life and rebuke that spirit because once there is fear, faith cannot rise and without faith, it is impossible to do anything that pleases God.

WORKSHEET

Your wife may have expressed some fears to you that you didn't take seriously. Can you recall some of them and begin to speak the word of God over them?

PRAYER POINTS

- Pray that she will not be a slave to fear, and she will have a constant consciousness that God is with her as a mighty Saviour.
- Pray that she will always be assured of God's love and with His love, He will calm all her fears.
- Pray that even though she walks through the darkest valley or extremely dangerous situations, she will fear no evil, for she will be conscious of the truth that you are with her.

- Pray that she will lie down every day with peace and that she will not have anything that will make her afraid.

DECLARATION

I declare that *(Insert your wife's name)* does not cower before any challenge or any person. She is bold and confident even in love. Fear and anxiety have no place in her. I declare that your word is always her first response. She recognizes the power that is at work in her and she uses that power. When fears and anxiety come knocking, she remembers to answer with Your Word. I declare that Your peace will guard her heart and mind. She is free from every spirit of fear, anxiety and doubt. Her eyes are fixed on You and not the circumstances around her, in Jesus Name.

FURTHER STUDY
Isaiah 41:10 (KJV) , Zephaniah 3:17 (NLT), Psalm 23:4 (NIV), Job 11:19 (NIV)

—09—
EYES THAT SEE

Ears that hear and eyes that see—we get our basic equipment from God!

—Proverbs 20:12 MSG

I'm sure you've figured out by now that I'm not just talking about physical eyes even though well, that's still kind of part of it right? Because it is important that your wife's eyes are functioning well but our prayer focus today is on discernment.

Just because someone has eyes doesn't mean they actually see and just because they have ears doesn't mean that they actually hear. Your wife naturally comes with intuition but you need her to be able to move it to discernment. She needs to be able to recognize good opportunities from bad but more importantly God opportunities from good ones. She needs to begin to see the way God sees and hear the way God hears.

The Bible tells us in Genesis 3:6 that Adam was with her when his wife was being deceived but he did nothing and 1 Timothy 2:14 confirms that he wasn't deceived. Today as husbands we will stand in the gap for our wives that they will be discerning when it comes to relationships, opportunities, timing, etc and she will hear God clearly.

WORKSHEET

Write out the areas you would like her to be more discerning in then create a schedule to remind your wife to pray in the Holy Ghost often.

_____
_____
_____
_____
_____
_____
_____
_____
_____

PRAYER POINTS

- Pray that God will open your wife's eyes so that she will not only see things from a natural perspective but she will become more discerning.
- Pray that God will open her eyes when she reads the scriptures so that she can truly see the marvellous things in His law.
- Pray that her eyes (both physical and spiritual) will no longer be closed, and her ears will listen and

hear what the Spirit is saying at all times.
- Pray that she will be discerning when it comes to relationships in your lives and be able to judge right from wrong.

DECLARATION

Heavenly Father, in Your infinite mercies, You have chosen to have a relationship with us, to instruct us in the way to go. Today, I declare that *(insert wife's name)* is discerning. The spirit of knowledge and understanding rests mightily upon her, that she knows precisely when something is from You, and when it is not. I declare that she obeys Your leading promptly. She has such discernment to not only make wise decisions but to also know she can trust Your guiding hand in Jesus Name.

FURTHER STUDY
Psalm 119:18 (NLT), Isaiah 32:3 (NIV)

—10—
SEASONED SPEECH

When she speaks she has something worthwhile to say, and she always says it kindly

—*Proverbs 31:26 MSG*

*I*f we would be very honest with ourselves, most of the time when we are arguing with our wives it is not just about what she's saying, it's about how she's saying it. No, let's be really honest, how many times have you said to yourself, "what she's saying makes sense but why would she talk to me like that? She has no respect!" and because of that, you miss out on some really great advice.

Most women have been known to be talkers so the issue isn't just about talking it's about how she talks. My wife used to have this challenge because she was very introverted and not so good with people, so she would have something worthwhile to say but the way she would say it was causing more harm than good as the person would not receive the advice or instruction because of how harshly it was coming out. Today just making that adjustment of speaking kindly, has changed her entire life and ministry. Pray for your wife that the way she speaks will not destroy her relationships.

WORKSHEET

Come up with a code that your wife would agree to and understand to mean a red flag or warning sign to stop talking.

PRAYER POINTS

- Pray that your wife will always have something important to say and that she will always say it kindly.
- Pray that no foul or polluting language, nor evil word nor unwholesome or worthless talk ever comes out of her mouth, but only speech that is good and beneficial to the spiritual progress of others, as is fitting to the need and the occasion, that it may be a

blessing and give God's favour to those who hear it.
- Pray that her words will always be fitly spoken; she will say the right things at the right time to the right person.
- Pray that she will always give great advice and that her speech will always be gracious, encouraging, inspiring, and seasoned with salt; she will always know how to speak to different people in their different seasons.

DECLARATION

I declare that *(insert your wife's name)* is graceful in how she handles bad situations. She is kind with her words and patient with others in their shortcomings. Her answers, regardless of the confrontation, are soft and so they turn away wrath. She is respectful, she is gentle and her words are seasoned with salt, they make anyone she speaks to a better person. Her speech, tone, choice of words and body language are anointed in Jesus name.

FURTHER STUDY
Ephesians 4:29 (AMPC), Proverbs 25:11 (ESV), Proverbs 15:23 (TPT),Colossians 4:6 (ESV)

—11—
RESTORED SOUL – AFTER ALL THE STRESS OF THE DAY

That's where he restores and revives my life. He opens before me the right path and leads me along in his footsteps of righteousness so that I can bring honour to his name

—Psalm 23:3 TPT

*L*ife has a way of draining us; whether you are male or female. Too many things happening at the same time; too many activities can often leave us burnt out. I believe that one of the greatest things you can do for your wife is to pray for her life to be restored and renewed, for her life to return daily.

Also because she multitasks, it's very easy for her to easily become overwhelmed or depleted. Not to mention the many different experiences she must have had in the marriage and in her life as a whole. Sometimes some negative experiences in the marriage keep coming up because it's eating at her. You need to pray that she will be able to let go of those things and that her soul will be restored. A restored soul means that she will not harbour bitterness, anger, and hatred or plan revenge. It also means that she will feel healthy emotions and be void of numbness or indifference. This means that her heart will find peace on a daily basis and she will be able to love you the way God expects her to.

WORKSHEET

List out the things that have been draining your wife in recent times or over the years and spend time praying for them to either be eliminated or strength and peace of mind to handle them.

What does she enjoy doing for relaxation? How can you be a part of making it happen more often for her?

PRAYER POINTS

- **Pray that God will restore and revive her life and**

that she will always bring honour to God's name.
- Pray that God will open before your wife the right path and lead her along in His footsteps of righteousness.
- Pray that your wife will always be renewed daily. Her body cells, systems and organs will function as though they were new.
- Pray that she will always remember to go to God whenever she feels overwhelmed and burdened so that He will cause her to rest.

DECLARATION

I declare that *(insert your wife's name)* is delivered from the many troubles of the world. Regardless of the chaos in her world, she will find rest in you Lord. I declare that she finds quiet in You in the midst of all the noise. She sleeps easily and wakes up refreshed everyday. Her mind is still and at peace not pacing about. Rather than focus on the negative, I declare that she is reminded of Your goodness and comfort at all times, in Jesus name.

FURTHER STUDY
Psalm 116:7 (NIV), Jeremiah 50:19 (NKJV), Psalm 68:19 (NKJV), Matthew 11:28 (AMPC)

—11—
NO SORROW

He will wipe every tear from their eyes, and there will be no more death or sorrow or crying or pain. All these things are gone forever

—Revelation 21:4 NLT

Have you ever heard your wife cry? Now, if you are the cause of those tears then maybe all you need to do is change not necessarily pray but if you have seen her encounter pain that you didn't cause or cannot necessarily do anything to ease then you know that you want to avoid it at all cost.

The reality of life is that bad things happen to good people; a concept that is sometimes hard to accept. They may encounter pain or sorrow from a miscarriage, infertility, loss of a loved one, loss of a job, or betrayal – the truth is bad things happen but more important is the fact that it can be avoided. You can avert disaster, sorrow and pain in her life and ask God for strength when they do happen for her to overcome the pain and declare that it will never happen again. I believe that as her husband you can tackle a lot of these things so they never happen and declare that she will see good all the days of her life on earth. She doesn't have to get to heaven for that to be her reality.

WORKSHEET

What are the internal causes of sorrow for your wife that you can avoid and what are the external causes that you can shield her from prayerfully?

PRAYER POINTS

- **Pray that God will wipe away every trace of sorrow or suffering in your wife's heart and in her life.**
- **Pray that pains from the past and present will be eradicated. That the Lord will be mighty in her life; He will save her from all forms of sorrow, and cause much rejoicing for her.**
- **Pray that violence shall no longer be heard in her land, neither wasting nor destruction. No longer**

will bad news be heard in her life. She will become a praise depot.

DECLARATION

I declare that *(insert your wife's name)* is far from sorrow and sorrow is far from her. She is delivered from disaster and pain. Her life will be evidence of Your goodness, Lord. For every pain she has encountered in the past, her heart is filled with hope and true faith. Every mourning is replaced with rejoicing and the ashes replaced with beauty. I declare that her heart is filled with Joy and Peace in Jesus Name.

FURTHER STUDY
Zephaniah 3:17 (KJV) Isaiah 60:18 (NKJV)

—13—
GRACE TO BUILD

A wise woman builds her home, but a foolish woman tears it down with her own hands.
—Proverbs 14:1 NLT

*T*his is probably one of the most quoted scriptures when it comes to the advice women get in marriage. And whether we like it or not the truth is most women are put under pressure to perform when they hear this. They feel like the responsibility of the marriage rests on them and they begin to feel overwhelmed.

Knowing this, pray for your wife to have the grace to build the home with you and the wisdom to know how to build the way God expects you both to. Any challenges she may encounter both from internal and external factors will be dealt with gracefully and with wisdom. She will have all that is required to help you build a home and a solid future together.

WORKSHEET

List out areas of your family that you need your wife to help you build.

Now declare strength over her and ask God to help her build correctly.

PRAYER POINTS

- Pray for your wife that she will be filled with wisdom and as a wise woman, she will build your home with you. She will not build with one hand and destroy with the other.
- Pray that she will be filled with grace and become an expert builder who will build carefully so that

the foundation she has laid, your children too will build their own lives and homes well.
- Pray that the LORD will make your wife like Rachel and Leah, who together built up the family of Israel. That she will be fruitful and have solid standing and be loved even in your extended family.
- Pray that she will surrender constantly to the real master builder to guide her in building right. For every house has a builder, but the one who built everything is God so she must trust God to build her home.

DECLARATION

Father I declare that *(insert your wife's name)* has the grace to build; our family, children, her career. She will live in the consciousness that You are the firm foundation and everything must be built on You. She does not rely on her understanding but in all her ways she acknowledges you and You direct her path. She is blessed with the wisdom and skills to fill our home with rare treasures. I declare that she is wise and all her decisions are sound in Jesus name.

FURTHER STUDY
1 Corinthians 3:10 (CEV), Ruth 4:11 (NIV), Hebrews 3:4 (NLT)

—14—
FRUITFUL VINE

Your wife will be like a fruitful vine within your house, your children will be like olive shoots around your table.

—*Psalm 128:3 NIV*

Every woman is created to be fruitful. In fact, that was God's command to mankind in Genesis. He said be fruitful and multiply. It was not a suggestion, it was a command. The woman was created as a man with a womb so that fruitfulness is something that is non-negotiable for her.

However, beyond the fruitfulness of having a child, you must pray that she will be fruitful in every area of her life. God's desire is that she will be fruitful irrespective of her age; fruitful in her body, her mind, her business, her ministry, her career, her relationships, etc. Fruitfulness means producing good results, to be beneficial; it means one is profitable. Fruitfulness also means to multiply or add to what is already existing, producing more of something. So if your wife is fruitful she multiplies what she already has and increases what you have. So whether it is having children to increase your family or having more money to increase your wealth, she needs to be fruitful.

WORKSHEET

What areas should your wife be displaying fruitfulness in? Find scriptures that promise fruitfulness and speak them over her daily.

What is she already fruitful at but can produce more?

PRAYER POINTS

- Pray that your wife will be like an olive tree flourishing in the house of God and trusting in God's unfailing love.
- Pray that she will stay fresh and green and will bear fruit even in old age.
- Pray that she will be like a tree planted by the rivers of water and she bears fruits in every area of her life in due season.

DECLARATION

I declare that *(insert your wife's name)* is fruitful in her body, mind, spirit, career, work, family and finances. Her land is bringing forth plenty, and her wells are bringing forth abundance of clean and fresh water. She will prosper and flourish in all she does. She will never know drought, famine or scarcity of anything. The wisdom of God is at work in her, producing excellence, success and prosperity in all of her endeavours.

FURTHER STUDY
Psalm 52:8 (NIV), Psalm 92:14 (NIV), Psalm 1:3 (KJV)

—15—
INNER STRENGTH

I pray that from his glorious, unlimited resources he will empower you with inner strength through his Spirit.

—*Ephesians 3:16 NLT*

As men, because we are so physical by nature, we tend to understand the importance of strength especially when it comes to physical strength. However, today our prayer focus is on inner strength. This will make sense to you when you consider that her body is not essentially her; she has what the Bible calls her inner man and that is the real person because the inner man, unlike the outer man does not die. So we need to invest prayer in strengthening her inner person.

Inner strength will cause her to have a strong spirit and ultimately translate to integrity of character; a resoluteness of will; which will birth a mental resistance to doubt or discouragement. When she has strength infused into her spirit by the Spirit of God she will be able to withstand pressures that are both external and internal because she can easily build her faith. Inner strength means she will have inner peace, quietness and confidence in such a turbulent world such as ours. This means she can face the future without any fear.

WORKSHEET

List areas of her life that drain her physically and possibly even emotionally then take time to strengthen by tackling them in prayer.

PRAYER POINTS

- Pray that your wife will not lose heart and that her inward man will be renewed day by day.
- Pray that your wife is empowered with inner strength through the Spirit of God.
- Pray that God will constantly give her power and where she is weakened and He will increase her strength.

DECLARATION

I declare that *(insert your wife's name)* is strengthened in her inner man by Your Spirit. Her mind is strengthened to overcome turmoil, confusion, and indecision. She has the strength to follow through on things she has started. The strength of the Lord is made manifest in her weakness. I declare that she is able to withstand any form of attack in Jesus name.

FURTHER STUDY
2 Corinthians 4:16 (NKJV) Isaiah 40:29 (ESV)

—16—
FINANCES

*And God is able to make all grace (every favor and [earthly blessing) come to you in abundance, so that you may always and under all circumstances
and whatever the need be self-sufficient [possessing enough to require no aid or support and furnished in abundance for every good work and charitable donation].*

—2 Corinthians 9:8 AMP

Money is important. I know I really don't have to tell you that and I'm sure you know that the presence or absence of money in a marriage plays a major part in the success of that marriage. Like I always say, in marriage, there's one person that must always be present at every meeting and called on for every major decision in the family and I'm sure we all know that "person" is money.

Everyone needs money whether male or female. Your wife needs money and not necessarily from you. The truth is everyone desires financial freedom such that they can bring their dreams to reality without begging or borrowing. For this to be possible in your wife's life, you have to realize that God is her source not you so you must pull on heavenly resources for all her bills to be paid and all her needs to be met.

Pray that she will also be blessed with financial clarity for multiple streams of income and ideas for generating passive income, at least on a monthly basis.

WORKSHEET

What can your wife do very well that she is not earning money from? How can you help her generate sales from this skill?

What problems are around her that she can provide solutions to?

What new skill, new course or certification can she acquire to start earning more?

_____
_____
_____
_____
_____
_____
_____
_____
_____

PRAYER POINTS

- Pray that God will give your wife the grace to be self-sufficient always and under all circumstances; that she will not need aid or support for any good work she decides to carry out or for any charitable donation.
- Pray that God will grant her abundant prosperity and she will get richer and richer by the day until she is very wealthy.
- Pray that the LORD will open the heavens, the storehouse of His bounty, to send rain on her land in season.

- Pray that your wife prospers in every currency of the world. That she is a money magnet.

DECLARATION

I declare that *(insert your wife's name)* prospers in all things, including her finances. The works of her hands are blessed and she experiences financial freedom. She has the wisdom to see and take on new opportunities for wealth generation. She will not only generate wealth but wisely invest and multiply it. She will lend to nations and borrow from none. I declare that she is sensitive to know when it is sowing time and what her seed is, and that her harvest will be bountiful in Jesus name.

FURTHER STUDY
Deuteronomy 28:11-12 (NIV), Genesis 24:53a (NIV), Genesis 26:13 (MSG)

—17—
MULTITASK EFFICIENTLY

She gets up while it is still night to prepare food for her family. She tells her servant women what they should do.

She thinks about a field and she buys it with her own money. And she plants fruit bushes to make wine. She is strong and she works well. She knows the cost of everything that she makes. And she works late into the night. She makes her own cloth from the beginning to the end.

She gives money to poor people. And she helps people that need help. All her family have warm clothes, so snow is not a problem.

—Proverbs 31:15-21 EASY

MULTITASK EFFICIENTLY

The Proverbs 31 woman is every man's dream – homely, street smart, entrepreneur, mother, wife, fashionable, spiritual, etc. She literally checked all the boxes. One of the things that is worthy of your attention is the fact that she was able to do all these things because she could multitask effectively.

The gift of multi-tasking, which is alien to most men, is actually a gift from God to women. It is kind of like having super powers. Our prayer focus today is that your wife will multitask effectively. She will not pack on more than she can handle or take on assignments that will destroy her health, family life or other projects. Her ability to also delegate effectively will enhance her multi-tasking so that she will get a lot done. It is also important for her to also be conscious of the fact that just because she can doesn't mean she should take on everything. She has to be like her master Jesus and only do what she sees the father do (John 5:19)

So it's not just about multi-tasking but multitasking effectively.

WORKSHEET

Write out the many things your wife has to handle in her life, especially day to day and take the time to pray for her to be able to juggle them all successfully.

What tasks do you think you should volunteer to help her with that can help make her life easier?

PRAYER POINTS

- Pray that your wife will not be overwhelmed by the multiple responsibilities and roles she has to play but the grace of God will enable her to carry them out effectively.
- Pray that she will be filled with the wisdom of God to know when and which tasks to delegate.
- Pray that God will strengthen her to do all the things she sets her heart to do.

DECLARATION

I declare that *(insert your wife's name)* comes to an understanding of how sophisticated she is and walks in fullness of that understanding. She is not limited in her thinking, therefore she is not limited in her abilities. I declare that as she juggles many tasks and projects, none of them will suffer or lack excellence. She is able to manage them all completely and none will suffer at the expense of another, for she can do all things through Christ who strengthens her in Jesus name.

FURTHER STUDY
Philippians 4:13 (NKJV), 1 Cor 15 :10 (NLT)

—18—
SHE WILL PROPHESY

And afterward I will pour out My Spirit upon all flesh; and your sons and your daughters shall prophesy, your old men shall dream dreams, your young men shall see visions.

—Joel 2:28 NIV

I've always found it rather fascinating that this scripture talks about the same spirit of God being poured out on all flesh yet it had different effects on different individuals. While the men expressed this encounter in dreams and visions, the women were to prophesy.

Now if you don't understand prophecy you may consider this a spooky prayer point but just follow me for a minute. Prophecy is simply inspired utterance, especially in line with declaring of the divine will and purpose of God or a prediction of something to come. Listen, I cannot tell you how many times I've been blessed by this particular gift. My wife would often come out of the place of prayer and tell me many things that the Spirit of God has revealed to her. Sometimes she reminds me of things I had said to her by declaring them to me again. The truth is your wife will speak whether you like it or not, your prayer should be that it will be inspired speech that reveals the heart of God.

WORKSHEET

Begin to take notes by writing down things that your wife says to you by the inspiration of the Holy Spirit that come to pass. Use this to boost her confidence in her ability to hear God and in speaking often.

PRAYER POINTS

- Pray that God will give your wife the ability to prophesy and she will not hold back due to fear.
- Pray that your wife will be a well-rounded woman like Deborah who was in marriage-a great wife, in business/career -successful judge and spiritually- a prophetess.
- Pray that she will always be filled with the Holy Ghost so she can prophesy boldly at all times.

DECLARATION

I declare that from today the spirit of prophecy rests on *(insert your wife's name).* I declare that her words are inspired by the Holy Ghost at every given moment. By the gift of prophecy, she will know Your purpose and will for her life, our family, and our children. The Spirit of truth will reveal to her things to come. She is strengthened in her walk of faith that she may believe, as the Spirit guides her into all the truth, in Jesus name.

FURTHER STUDY
1 Corinthians 12:10a (NLT) Judges 4:4 (ESV) Luke 1:67 (BSB)

—19—
HER UNDERSTANDING ENLIGHTENED
(UNDERSTANDING THE CALL OF GOD ON HER LIFE)

I pray that the Father of glory, the God of our Lord Jesus Christ, would impart to you the riches of the Spirit of wisdom and the Spirit of revelation to know him through your deepening intimacy with him. I pray that the light of God will illuminate the eyes of your imagination, flooding you with light, until you experience the full revelation of the hope of his calling—that is, the wealth of God's glorious inheritances that he finds in us, his holy ones!
I pray that you will continually experience the immeasurable greatness of God's power made available to you through faith. Then your lives will be an advertisement of this immense power as it works through you!
—Ephesians 1:17-19 TPT

*E*very child of God is born with a purpose. In fact Jeremiah chapter 1 verse 5 tells us that even before God formed us He knew us and ordained us. Everyone has a destiny in God that must be fulfilled. Your prayer is for light to come so your wife can have a clear understanding of what she was born to do.

The kind of light that will bring illumination so that she will be aware of the great power of God that is available to her and will use that power to do great things. Light and clarity are two major factors in her fulfilling destiny. She will see and have a very clear understanding of her "what", "why", "how", "where" and "when". Once she gets a grip on the assignment, she can fully carry it out and in turn, be an advertisement of what God can do with a life that is surrendered to him.

Her greatest satisfaction will come from walking in purpose; of knowing she's doing what she was born to do.

WORKSHEET

What things do you think your wife is called to do with her life? Write them down and take the time to pray for clarity for her so that she can see it as her life's calling and pursue it accordingly.

PRAYER POINTS

- Pray that the light of God will illuminate the eyes of your wife's imagination, flooding her with light, until she experiences the full revelation of the hope of His calling so that she can understand and follow that path fully.
- Pray that she will continually experience the

immeasurable greatness of God's power made available to her through faith.
- Pray that the eyes of her understanding are open so that she might understand the scriptures when she studies them.
- Pray that the Lord reveals profound mysteries beyond man's understanding to her.

DECLARATION

I declare over *(insert your wife's name)*, that her eyes will be open to know Your plans and purpose for her. She is not consumed with the many activities around her, but she knows exactly what You have called her to do. I declare that the eyes of her understanding are open to see the gifts and talents You have given her and how to use them for Your purpose. She follows Your will wholeheartedly. Her mind is illuminated and void of confusion in Jesus name.

FURTHER STUDY
Luke 24:45 (KJV) Daniel 2:22 (TLB)

—20—
UNHOLY ALLIANCES

Blessed (happy, fortunate, prosperous, and enviable) is the man who walks and lives not in the counsel of the ungodly [following their advice, their plans and purposes], nor stands [submissive and inactive] in the path where sinners walk, nor sits down [to relax and rest] where the scornful [and the mockers] gather. But his delight and desire are in the law of the Lord, and on His law (the precepts, the instructions, the teachings of God) he habitually meditates (ponders and studies) by day and by night.

—Psalm 1: 1-2 AMPC

Generally, women are thought to be more relational than men so I believe they thrive on having lots of relationships. That in itself is not bad when they are not unholy alliances.

Personally, relationships are very valuable to me. I don't believe people should not have friends and I'm not expecting you to begin to monitor every one in your wife's life but your job as her husband is to protect her by praying against relationships that may affect her heart towards God, your marriage and your future together.

This scripture is clear on the kind of people she needs to avoid – those who give evil advice, those who live like sinners, those who make fun of God and the things of God. The Bible is clear on the fact that anyone found in these circles would not be blessed.

So if you want a happy, fortunate, prosperous, and enviable wife, my advice is to address this in the place of prayer. Most men try to enforce this by setting rules and putting their foot down. I find that really amusing because if you even succeed at bullying your wife into subservience, you will still be stuck with a miserable wife. My advice is to pray for the right relationships in her life.

WORKSHEET

Which of her friends have you identified to be a negative influence in her life and why? Write out the reasons and if she is already exhibiting any of the negative attributes, pray them out of her life.

PRAYER POINTS

- Pray that she will not be unequally yoked with unbelievers and will not be comfortable in an alliance with them.
- Pray that she will be able to discern unholy relationships, fellowships, meetings, etc and stay away from them.
- Pray that she will be firm and graced to say NO

to enticements from sinners or ungodly men and women.
- Pray that your wife will be so comfortable in God's presence that she will automatically repel bad relationships if they attempt to come up in her life.

DECLARATION

I declare that *(insert your wife's name)* is surrounded by people who will build her up. Her support system is built by you. She attracts only good company. She reviews her circle and lets go of relationships that will harm her or bring her negative counsel. I declare that she is able to discern and choose who she lets into her space. She is not blinded by sentiments or the need to please anyone. She knows where to draw the line and set boundaries in Jesus name.

FURTHER STUDY
Isaiah 8:12 (HCSB) 2Cor 6:14 (NIV) Proverbs 1:10 (ESV)

—21—
HER CONVERSATIONS

Now the serpent was more crafty than any of the wild animals the Lord God had made. He said to the woman, "Did God really say, 'You must not eat from any tree in the garden'?"

—*Genesis 3:1 NIV*

First Corinthians 15:33 tells us, ***Don't fool yourselves. Bad friends will destroy you.***

The relationships in your wife's life have the power to affect her life in totality. It's never really harmless.

I'm sure when satan began a conversation with Eve she never thought it would result in her losing her place in Eden and ruining the lives of all of mankind. It seemed like a harmless relationship. In fact, I don't think it was a one off conversation. Perhaps they had been talking because she didn't seem alarmed by the conversation. She seemed very comfortable. That is one of the reasons satan was able to worm his way into her heart – relationship.

Listening to the wrong people can make your wife begin to question the values you both already have. Usually when a couple comes into a counselling session, and the man complains that his wife has changed, we can usually trace it back to whom she's talking to and the company she's keeping. So praying about your wife's circle is not negotiable especially because the decisions she makes has a way of affecting you too. You don't agree? Ask Adam.

WORKSHEET

Write out the people your wife spends time with the most. Are they godly relationships?

PRAYER POINTS

- Pray that your wife will not be persuaded by wrong friendship to lose her confidence and trust in God.
- Pray that your wife will not heed the voices of deception around her but will rebuke them whenever they speak.
- Pray that the voice of the Holy Spirit will always be louder than the voice of the enemy.
- Pray that she will not be deceived or lured into negative habits that can destroy your home or her life.

DECLARATION

I declare that *(insert your wife's name)* is unresponsive to negative voices around her. She only listens to voices that don't stray from your precepts. I declare that she is disciplined in her conversations and her words are seasoned with salt. She does not walk in the counsel of the ungodly or sit in the seat of the scornful. I silence every voice of destruction and deceit and replace them with voices of godly counsel in Jesus name.

FURTHER STUDY
Isaiah 36: 13-20 (NIV) Job 2:9-10 (NLT) 2Timothy 1:13

—22—
PILLAR NOT A CATERPILLAR

*That our daughters may be as pillars,
Sculptured in palace style;*

—Psalm 144:12b NKJV

To really understand today's prayer focus, you need to think of your marriage as a building. Our scripture for today describes our wives as pillars sculpted in palace style. For you to really appreciate this you need to first consider what a pillar does in a house.

A pillar is a firm integral upright support for a superstructure and joins walls together. In this case your wife is that pillar; she is the support for the family unit. She unites the family, as a cornerstone, she joins everyone together, and at the same time she adorns the home the same way polished stones garnish the structure into which they are built.

Today let us pray for the grace required for your wife to uphold the family as a support, let us pray that her strength will not fail her and that she will do it gracefully.

WORKSHEET

List out some things that your wife does to support the family. Now acknowledge and appreciate her for these things and pray for her to have the strength to keep doing them.

PRAYER POINTS

- Pray that the Lord will make your wife like a fortified city, an iron pillar and a bronze wall of unflinching support to your family.
- Pray that her default clothing will be strength and dignity leaving no room for fear or errors because she will always be secure.
- Pray that there will be no cracks in her character so that she can play her role as a pillar.

—23—
HELP

> "But you, Israel, are my servant. You're Jacob, my first choice, descendants of my good friend Abraham. I pulled you in from all over the world, called you in from every dark corner of the earth, telling you, 'You're my servant, serving on my side. I've picked you. I haven't dropped you. Don't panic. I'm with you. There's no need to fear for I'm your God. I'll give you strength. I'll help you. I'll hold you steady, keep a firm grip on you.
>
> —*Isaiah 41:8-10 MSG*

*E*veryone needs help. I know your wife was created to be your helper but news flash- she too needs help. And yes she needs help from you but she also needs help in areas you cannot provide help. So what do you do? You hand her over to the one that can help her.

God's promise is that He will be with her; He will give her strength and more importantly that He will help her. Pray that your wife will never lack the help that she needs - whether physical, emotional or physical, and that she will be marvellously helped by God. She will receive this help from men sent by God, from angels assigned to her and from God himself.

Interestingly, sometimes she may not even know that what she needs is help and maybe you have watched her struggle unnecessarily especially if you are married to a hardworking woman with a knack for martyrdom, let me tell you, you need to insist that she gets help and that she will recognize and accept the help when it does come and when it is offered. I know this is hard for you to understand because you are not averse to getting help but sometimes some women struggle with it. The easiest way to ensure she gets help and it doesn't become a fight is to address it in prayer.

WORKSHEET

What activities has your wife gotten involved in that have caused her to burn out? How can you step in to ensure this does not re-occur?

_____
_____
_____
_____
_____
_____
_____
_____

What will make her life easier? Is it a piece of equipment? When will you get it for her?

_____
_____
_____
_____
_____

PRAYER POINTS

- Pray that your wife will never lack the help that she needs - whether physical, emotional or spiritual,

that she will always be marvellously helped by God and it will come on time.
- Pray that because God is in the midst of her, she will not be moved by situations or unforeseen events when they arise. She will set her face like a flint knowing she can never be disgraced.
- Pray that she will not be afraid of people's opinions but will be confident in the truth that God will never leave her nor forsake her and neither will she see shame all the days of her life.
- Pray that she recognizes help when it comes and that she will be willing to accept it.

DECLARATION

I declare today that *(insert your wife's name)*, is marvellously helped by You. In every area where she needs help, she will not lack it. She will be open to receiving help rather than struggle to do things on her own. Even at times when she does not acknowledge that she needs help, You will send helpers her way and she will recognize them. When she is at a crossroads, rather than slip into fear, she will lift up her eyes to you from whence her help comes from.

FURTHER STUDY
Isaiah 50:7 (NKJV) Psalm 46:5 (NKJV) Hebrews 13:6 (AMP) Psalm 91:14 (AMP)

—24—
PEACE AND NO WORRY

Peace I leave with you; My [own] peace I now give and bequeath to you. Not as the world gives do I give to you. Do not let your hearts be troubled, neither let them be afraid. [Stop allowing yourselves to be agitated and disturbed; and do not permit yourselves to be fearful and intimidated and cowardly and unsettled.]

—*John 14:27 AMPC*

Life happens and the truth is we cannot always predict the future but there are two things I know will always come whether we like it or not – challenges and opportunities. Now what we can control however is the way we react to these challenges.

Your wife will be tempted to give into worry sometimes and what that does is that it introduces anxiety and anxiety will cause her to lose her peace. God is very clear on how He feels about anxiety, fear and worry; He doesn't want it anywhere near His children. God gives peace and that is what your wife needs. Peace is not necessarily the absence of stress or trouble, it is the consciousness of God and the fact that He sustains, no matter the circumstance. Your desire is that she will stop allowing herself to be agitated and disturbed; and she will not permit herself to be fearful, intimidated, cowardly or unsettled.

Pray that she will have the peace that God gives, the kind that passes all understanding.

WORKSHEET

What are the things that cause your wife to lose her peace? Find God's promises on it and insist on them becoming a reality in her life.

PRAYER POINTS

- **Pray that your wife will not be pulled in different directions or worried about anything. Rather, she will be saturated in prayer throughout each day.**
- **Pray that God's wonderful peace that transcends human understanding, will guard her heart and mind as she goes about her daily activities.**
- **Pray that regardless of life's circumstances, the Lord of peace Himself will grant her His peace at all times and in every way.**

DECLARATION

I declare that *(insert your wife's name)* enjoys your peace. Not the kind the world gives but your peace that passes all understanding. I rebuke every spirit of fear, timidity, anxiety and unrest. I declare that she has strength and clarity of mind and that she trusts that You are working every little detail of her life out for her good. She is not tossed about by the events around her but she stands firm on your word from where her confidence comes. Her knowledge of Your word gives her power and a sound mind in Jesus name.

FURTHER STUDY
Philippians 4:6-7 (TPT), 2Thessalonians 3:16 (AMP)

—25—
NONE OF THESE DISEASES

And said, If thou wilt diligently hearken to the voice of the LORD thy God, and wilt do that which is right in his sight, and wilt give ear to his commandments, and keep all his statutes, I will put none of these diseases upon thee, which I have brought upon the Egyptians: for I am the LORD that healeth thee.

—Exodus 15:26 KJV

The Israelites had seen the Egyptians inflicted with all kinds of diseases. They encountered first hand what it meant to be on God's opposing side. After they left Egypt, God gave them instructions on how to make sure that they would not live a life where these diseases would be visited on them.

Today our prayer focus is that your wife will listen to God's instructions and obey them. Sometimes the instructions may not necessarily be spiritual instructions, they may be physical instructions like rest, eat healthy, etc but if she follows them the end result is health. She will also be exempt from any sickness that is affecting others. The covenant of health is hers.

WORKSHEET

Help your wife find healing scriptures that she can confess day and night and ensure she takes her daily dose of God's medicine (healing scriptures).

PRAYER POINTS

- Pray that as your wife serves God, He will bless her bread and water; she will not be allergic to any foods and He will take all sickness away from her.
- Pray that no terrible disaster will strike her and your home as God's word has become a shield for her and all that is hers.
- Pray that evil shall not come near her and disease shall not come near her dwelling.

- Pray that God will cause her to enjoy a long and full life.

DECLARATION

I declare that *(insert your wife's name)* suffers no disease. Because she serves You, her food and her water is blessed. Whatever she ingests provides nourishment to her body. Because You protect her, not one of her bones shall be broken. Your word is healing to her flesh. I declare that even if she takes any poisonous substance, it will by no means harm her. No infection comes near her dwelling in Jesus name.

FURTHER STUDY
Exodus 23:25 KJV), Psalm 91:10 (CEV), Psalm 91:10 (ABPE)

—26—
CALL HER BLESSED

Her children rise up and call her blessed; Her husband also, and he praises her.

—Proverbs 31:28 NKJV

*E*very woman's dream is to see her children rise in life and be the best at whatever they do. This is the reason why they invest time, energy and prayers into them.

Most women would give anything to see that their children are doing well or to ensure that they don't lack anything. One of the most heartbreaking things for them would be after they have worked so hard their children don't rise to great heights or they lose their relationship with their children.

My prayer for my wife which should also be yours for your wife is that our children will rise to exceed even her wildest dreams for them and that they will recognize the sacrifices she made and honour her for it. My prayer is that my children rise up and call her blessed and I will have no choice but to join them because she would have proven herself to be an exceptional mum. I think that should be your prayer too.

WORKSHEET

What can you do to foster more love between your wife and your children?

What ways can you train and help your children to honour their mother ?

PRAYER POINTS

- **Pray that her children will find solace in her and see her as a role model they can look up to.**

- Pray that she would do excellently well in her job of raising godly seeds.
- Pray that her children will speak with the enemy at the gate and always refer to her words of wisdom, correction, advice and instructions.
- Pray that she will skillfully guide her children like arrows into fulfilling destiny.
- Pray that she will partner effectively with God in her divine assignment of parenting.

DECLARATION

I declare that *(insert your wife's name)* enjoys our children. They will be a source of joy for her. They will defend her at the city gates. Our children make her proud beyond her wildest imaginations, I declare that she is respected and honoured amongst her peers on account of her children's excellence. As they soar high, they will remain rooted in God and connected to their home and honour her. I declare that she is blessed to raise them right, and when they rise they will call her blessed in Jesus name.

FURTHER STUDY
Isaiah 60:4 (The Voice), Genesis 17:16 (TLB), Genesis 17:16 (NLT)

—27—
EXEMPT FROM HUSTLE

The blessing of the Lord brings wealth, without painful toil for it.

—Proverbs 10:22 NIV

I often hear people brag about hustling; they talk about the hustle life like it is something to be proud of. Now don't get me wrong I understand that all these are said with the context of working hard but you must also understand that as a believer there are some concepts that may sound cool but are actually not for us as believers.

The first mention of hustle was when Adam and Eve sinned. Before that, they understood what it was like to be taken care of by God. They enjoyed the beauty of work minus the hustle. God blessed their work. After they sinned, things became different; they literally had to hustle before getting anything. Jesus came to restore us back to that state of blessing where we don't have to suffer before we are blessed. That blessing is the type that comes only from God and it isn't with hard labour; no sorrow is added to it.

As a husband, declare over your wife that God will bless her work so that it will bring wealth and she will not damage her health in the process of getting rich.

WORKSHEET

What does your wife do for a living? How can she do better? Write out what success would mean for her and how she can achieve this with minimal effort because the blessing will be at work.

What platforms can you explore to help raise the visibility of your wife's business or services to potential clients and if she is a career person, what can she do to become better qualified for opportunities?

PRAYER POINTS

- Pray that she will always be conscious of the blessing of God already at work in her life.
- Pray that the blessing of the Lord will enrich your wife with results that will make her attract material blessings without struggling.
- Pray that the Blessing will give her exponential increase from fields others have laboured in because she will reap from them.
- Pray that she will take a mental position of rest which provokes the blessing of being blessed even in your sleep.

DECLARATION

I declare that the works of *(insert your wife's name)* hands are blessed. Every effort she puts in will yield results. She walks in consciousness of the blessing of the Lord that makes rich without painful toil for it. I declare that she is protected from the worries of the day and the fears of the night. She relies on Your sufficient strength and promised grace in Jesus Name.

FURTHER STUDY
John 4:38 (NIV), Psalm 127v2b (AMPC)

—28—
HEALTH AND HEALING

For I will restore health to you and heal you of your wounds,' says the Lord,

—Jeremiah 30:17 NKJV

As we've established earlier, God's desire for your wife goes beyond healing when she's sick to her actually walking in divine health. God really wants your wife not to even fall ill at all.

However, today's prayer focus moves beyond that to wounds. What is a wound? Simply put, it is an injury to a living tissue caused by a cut, blow, or other impact, typically one in which the skin is cut or broken. Interestingly your wife may have many wounds over the years some physical and some emotional and these are the ones we choose to focus on today.

I'm sure you know that many things may have cut her or bruised her in life and possibly in the marriage. Words or things that may have happened may have left wounds in her and she has refused to let go of the pain. Pray that the lord would heal her of every wound whether physical or emotional, give her the strength to forgive and restore her to health.

WORKSHEET

Help her identify people or acts she needs to forgive and encourage her to let go of the offence.

PRAYER POINTS

- Pray that the Lord will restore health to your wife and heal her of all her emotional wounds.
- Pray that the Lord will heal her and reveal to her the abundance of peace and security available to her.
- Pray that the Lord will bless her bread and her water, and He will take sickness away from the midst of her.

DECLARATION

Today I declare that every promise on health, healing and restoration is manifested in *(insert your wife's name)* life. She understands and walks in divine health. Her organs function optimally. In her soul, she is healthy. In her mind, she is healthy. In her body, she is healthy. I declare that she is replenished with new strength every morning. She suffers no disease as her heart is open to your word and it's healing power. The same spirit that raised Jesus from the dead lives within her, so her mortal body is quickened in Jesus name.

FURTHER STUDY
Jeremiah 33:6 (ESV), Exodus 23:25 (NKJV) , Isaiah 58:8 (ESV), 1 Peter 2:4

—29—
EVERY NEED SUPPLIED

I pray that God will take care of all your needs with the wonderful blessings that come from Christ Jesus!

—Philippians 4:19 CEV

*E*very woman, secretly in her heart has this one desire: she wants to relax and be taken care of and if we are really being honest, even if you want to try, you cannot take care of all her needs.

Women have many needs and sadly most men just assume that once they have provided financially, all the woman's needs have been met. Trust me, you haven't even begun to scratch the surface of her needs. A woman is so multidimensional, that is why you can never even figure out all her needs in the first place. However God can; he knows her and he gets her. He has promised to meet all her needs, and listen with God, all means all; you don't have to worry about anything being left out.

So simply hand her over to her heavenly father to take care of all her needs.

WORKSHEET

What needs has your wife communicated to you recently? Pray that the Lord will meet those needs either through you or any other source He deems fit.

Now, tick the ones you can handle and commit the others you cannot handle to God in prayer.

PRAYER POINTS

- **Pray that God will take care of all your wife's needs according to His riches in glory.**
- **Pray that the Lord will open His Hand and satisfy all of her desires and even exceed them.**
- **Pray that she walks in the consciousness of the Lord being her shepherd, so she has all she needs.**

DECLARATION

I declare that *(insert your wife's name)* needs are always met and on time. Her heart is rid of fear, anxiety, worry, and doubt when she is in need, instead, her eyes are fixed on Your riches in glory. I declare that she walks in divine abundance and that the mindset of lack is far from her. Every project she sets out to do is adequately provided for and she is able to carry them out.

FURTHER STUDY
Psalm 145:16 (AMP), Psalm 23:1 (CEV)

—30—
EVEN WHEN SHE SLEEPS

Without the help of the LORD, it is useless to build a home or to guard a city.

It is useless to get up early and stay up late in order to earn a living. God takes care of his own, even while they sleep.

—Psalm 127: 1-2 CEV

My wife always seems to be on the move; always doing something for God, for me, for the children and for a lot of other people. Her life is very busy and sometimes I think she feels the need to keep going because she feels like a lot of things are resting on her.

One thing I do know is that if she gets into that mode of trying to make things happen on her own, it would become a disaster. My prayer is that she learns to rest in God knowing that without Him whatever she's trying to make happen will not.

I believe that this is a very important prayer focus because the three things mentioned here are the three things women try to achieve- they try to build their homes, they often feel like they are gatekeepers of the home and try to guard their families, they also want to make a living but God has a better way to ensure she has all these without being stressed.

WORKSHEET

Create a time table of scheduled rest for your wife weekly and make a commitment to helping her rest by planning family and couple getaways as often as you can.

PRAYER POINTS

- Pray that your wife will receive provision even when she is not working and money will be flowing to her even while she sleeps.
- Pray that she will be like a well-watered garden flourishing on every side because the Lord Himself waters her.

DECLARATION

Lord, You designed us for rest, so I declare that, *(insert your wife's name)* would follow Your example of work and rest. I declare that every minute of rest that she has is multiplied. She is filled with the wisdom to know when and how to rest in You. She understands the importance of taking time off and has the grace and discipline to choose rest over worry, in Jesus name Amen.

FURTHER STUDY
Matthew 11:28 (NLT), Matthew 6:31-32 (AMP)

—31— A GUARDED HEART

Guard your heart above all else, for it determines the course of your life.

—Proverbs 4:23 NLT

The Bible says in Ecclesiastes 7:8, that better is the end of a thing than the beginning; today our prayer focus may actually be the most important even if it is the last one. So this is the last one but by no means the least.

I believe that the core of everything is the heart. Even our scripture focus for today is very clear on the fact that God wants us to guard our hearts or watch over our hearts diligently because it determines the course of our lives and everything we do flows from it. Knowing this, our focus today will be on praying for your wife's heart. Her heart should be preserved, kept pure and tender towards God and the things of God.

Our prayer today is that her heart will be malleable in God's hand, that she will not have room for evil thoughts, jealousy, bitterness, and all other negative emotions. That her heart will stay beautiful and pure towards God and men.

WORKSHEET

List practical ways you can help to keep your wife's heart focused on God.

PRAYER POINTS

- Pray that your wife will not be afraid of evil tidings or bad news because God gives her a steadfast heart, a heart that trusts wholly in Him in all things.
- Pray that God will remain the strength of her heart and her portion forever. That her heart will stay beautiful and pure towards God and men.
- Pray that she will not have room for evil thoughts, jealousy, bitterness, and all other negative emotions.
- Pray that when God tests her heart she will not be

found wanting. Instead, God will reward her for all her labour of love.

DECLARATION

I declare that *(insert your wife's name)* heart is preserved and kept pure. She produces only good things because her heart is good. Her heart is not hardened; therefore, she is able to receive instructions and corrections from God. The Lord remains the strength of her heart forever, in Jesus name.

FURTHER STUDY
Psalm 73:26 (NIV), Psalm 112:7 (NKJV), Luke 6:45 (NLT), Jeremiah 17:10 (NIV)

—BONUS—
A FAITHFUL WIFE

> *Charm can mislead and beauty soon fades. The woman to be admired and praised is the woman who lives in the Fear-of-God.*
>
> *—Proverbs 31:30 MSG*

I've been a marriage counsellor for over 25 years and you'll be shocked to know that in today's world and in my counselling experience, married women also are unfaithful to their partners. I dare say even more than men which shows that contrary to what most people believe women are just as susceptible to the deception of satan when it comes to infidelity.

Your wife will meet all kinds of men at her work place, church, business arena and everywhere she goes. She can even run into men from her past life and you won't always be there. So she has to be the kind of woman who cannot be swayed by the deception of satan through the subtle wiles of men ....*or women.*

Your prayer is that your wife will honour her marriage vows first to God, to keep her body holy, her thoughts pure and her actions will be in agreement with her commitment to keep the marriage bed undefiled.

WORKSHEET

Write out ten things you love about your wife. Find ways to always remind yourself and her about these qualities. Compliment her regularly

----

Pick a day in the month for reminding yourselves of your marriage vows and another day for a date night

----

PRAYER POINTS

- **Pray that your wife will be faithful to the covenant of marriage and she will always remember the vows she made before God.**

- Pray that your wife will not be deceived or swayed by men that come to her in all forms.
- Pray that she will be strong enough to resist temptations that come her way from men she meets as she goes about her work and assignment.
- Pray that she has the wisdom to keep herself so the evil one will not touch her.

DECLARATION

I declare that *(insert your wife's name)* is a faithful wife to me. She is a loyal wife who has integrity and walks in the fear of God. She keeps herself and the devil does not touch her. I declare that she has the spirit of discernment to recognise deceitful men that have hidden motives to lure her into sin. I declare that she will never fall prey to them. *(Insert your wife's name)* is full of wisdom and honours God in her thoughts, conversations and actions. I declare that because she loves God above all things, she will remain faithful to our marriage covenant as a commitment firstly to honour God, and the love we share.

FURTHER STUDY
1st Timothy 3:11 (CSB), Proverbs 31:10-12 (NIV), 1 John 5:18 (BSB)

AUTHOR'S PROFILE

Kingsley Okonkwo is a Specialist when it comes to Relationships and Marriages. With over two decades hands-on experience as a pastor, relationship coach, counsellor and best-selling author, PK, as he is fondly called is a presidential member of the American Association of Christian Counsellors, a board-certified Master Christian Life Coach and a certified relationship counsellor. He is renowned for Love and Relationships, Marriage and Family Life, Domestic Violence, Divorce and Infidelity Recovery.

He is the visionary behind the phenomenal Love, Dating and Marriage Ministry, widely known as Ldmwithpk, a highly impactful relationship ministry with a reach of hundreds of thousands of people across the globe. Kingsley Okonkwo is committed to equipping couples around the world with godly principles for building strong relationships and marriages having lived on the same principles himself for close to two decades. He is convinced that godliness is the foundation for quarrel-free marriages and as such hosts the Together Forever conference an annual Interdenominational event for married couples aimed at rekindling the passion and love in marriages.

Notably, his ministry records mind blowing

Author's Profile

testimonies of blissful relationships and marriages to the glory of God as more single people find the right partners, troubled marriages experience total restoration, individuals are delivered from sexual addictions and wrong mindsets redirected. His unique say-it-as-it-is, fun-filled style of teaching God's principles for dating, courtship and marriage endears him to both the young and old as they are greatly impacted by his relationship masterclasses, one-on-one coaching classes, live broadcasts on social media and numerous ministry resources.

Pastor Kingsley continues to be a blessing across continents through itinerant relationship seminars, conferences and counselling sessions across Canada, United States of America, United Kingdom, the Middle East and numerous African countries. His messages and ministry materials are highly sought- after around the globe. He has authored numerous books on relationships, a few of which he co-authored with his lovely wife and partner in ministry, Pastor Mildred and they are blessed with three adorable children.

resources

ALL YEAR ROUND FOR MEN

ALL YEAR ROUND FOR MEN is a 52-WEEK GUIDE ON HOW TO LOVE YOUR WIFE. It is a practical, and easy-to-follow companion for the husband who wants to do right by his wife, making her feel special, loved and protected. It contains 52 tested and trusted tips to help you love your wife all year round.

OTHER BOOKS BY KINGSLEY & MILDRED OKONKWO

- All Year Round- For Men
- A-Z Of Marriage
- 7 Things I Badly Want To Tell Women
- Praying For Your Husband
- When Am I Ready?
- Who Should I Marry?
- 25 Wrong Reasons People Enter Relationships.
- Just Us Girls
- I Love You But My Parents Say No
- Should Ladies Propose?
- God Told Me To Marry You
- Waiting For Isaac
- 7 Questions Wise Women Ask
- 7 Qualities Wise Men Want
- Chayil- The Virtuous Woman
- Help! My Husband Is Acting Funny
- All Year Round- For Women
- Hannah's Heart Devotional
- Manual- The Way Men think
- One Thing
- God Can Be Trusted- Volume 1 & 2
- How to Know If He or She Really Loves You

Made in the USA
Middletown, DE
07 February 2025

70460451R00115